ACTION   ACTION   ACTION

ALL GIRL

ACTION

THE PSOE RECOURSE BOOK FOR THE COMIC BOOK ARTIST

This book is designed for the comic
book artist that want to draw women
but have a hard time getting it right.
This book is filled with no nonsense
straight to the point easy to follow
drawings of women in action poses
for you or anyone to draw.
This is not only a great source reference
book, it also makes for a wonderful
drawing practice book as well.

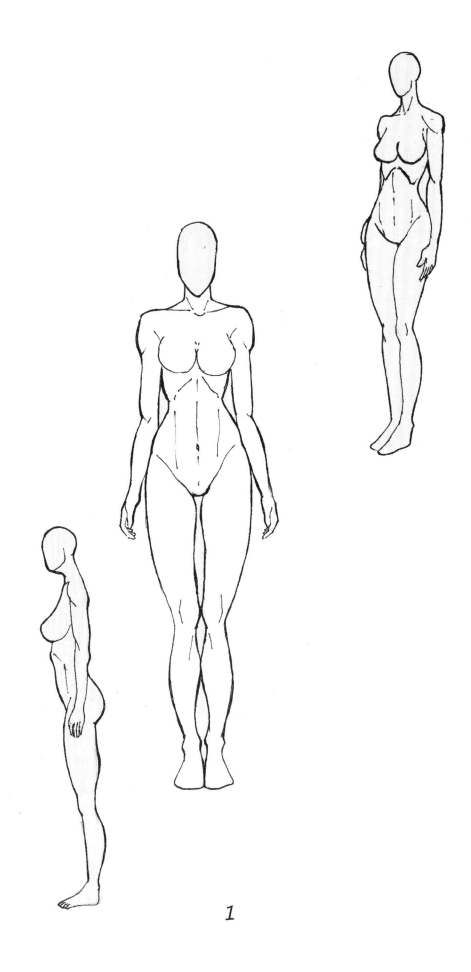

1

2

3

4

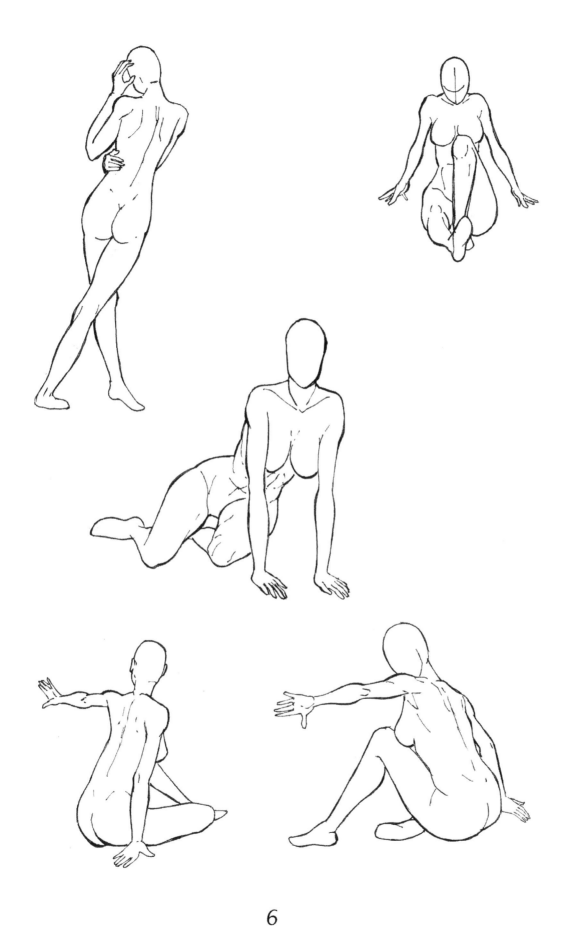

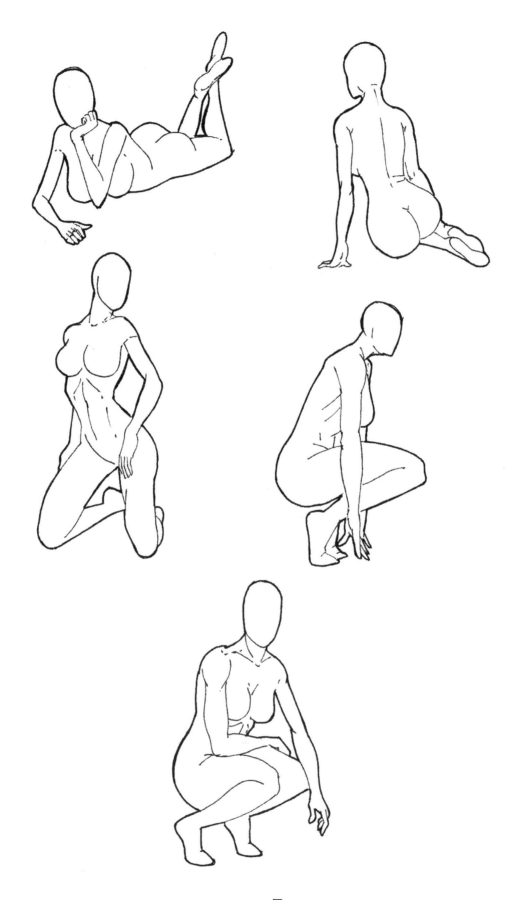

8

9

10

11

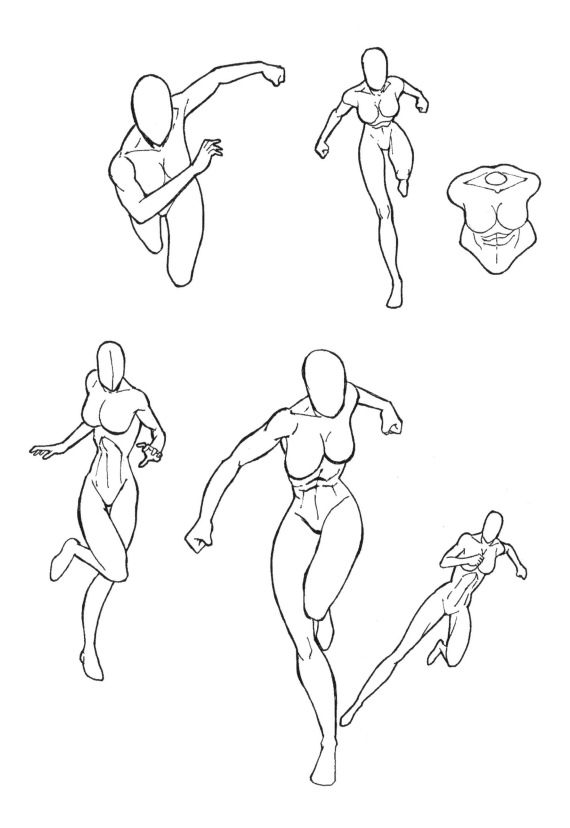

12

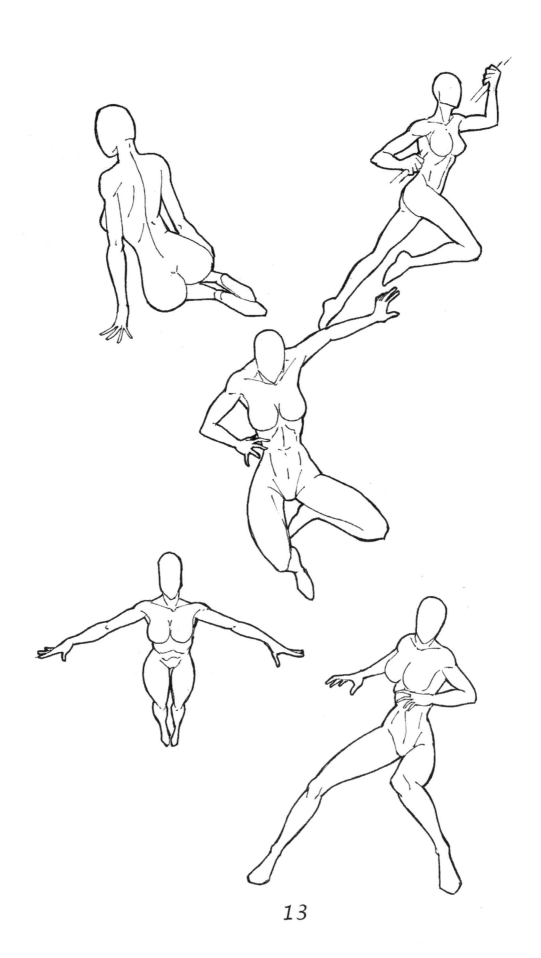

13

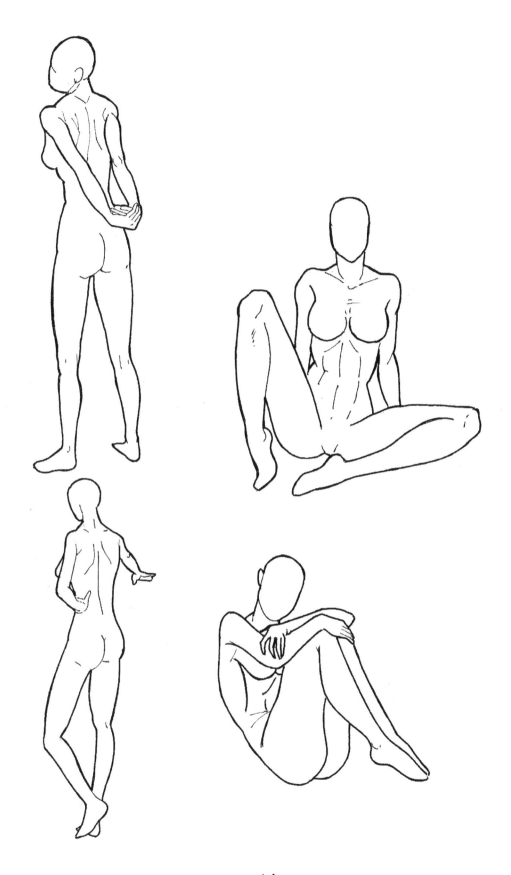

14

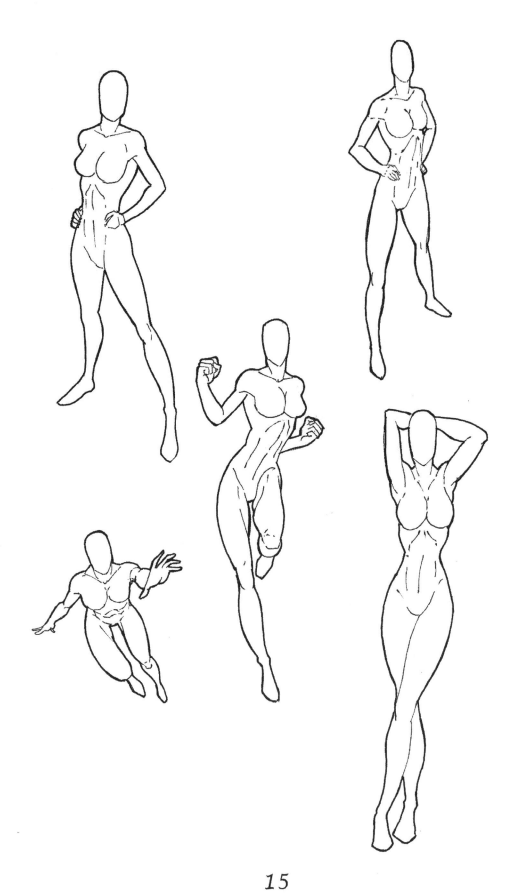

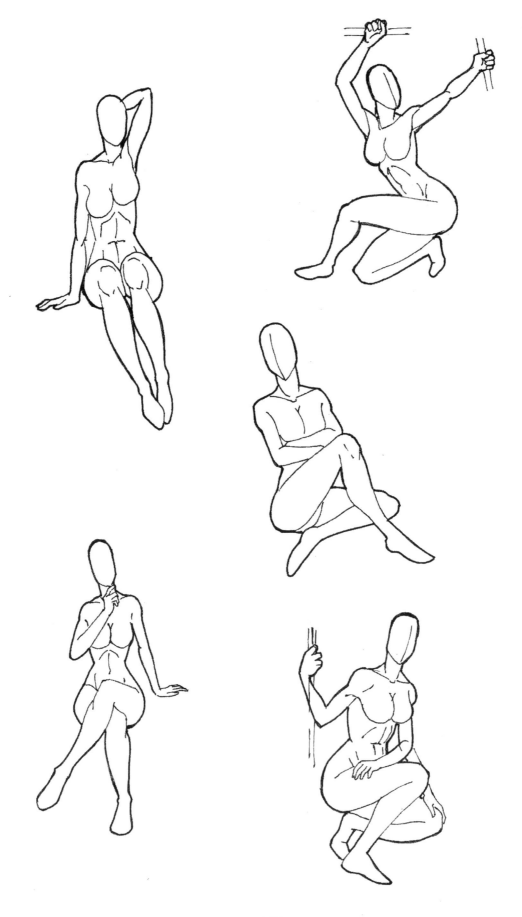

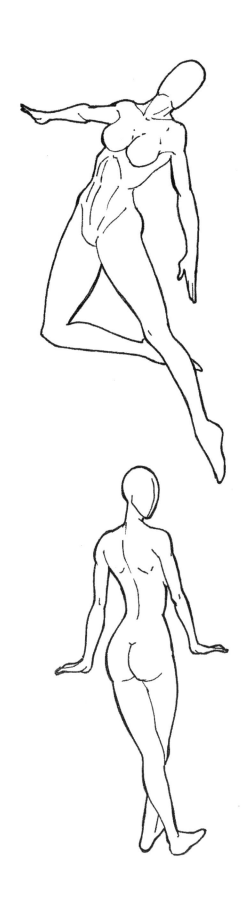
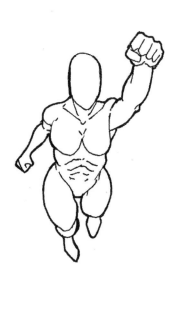

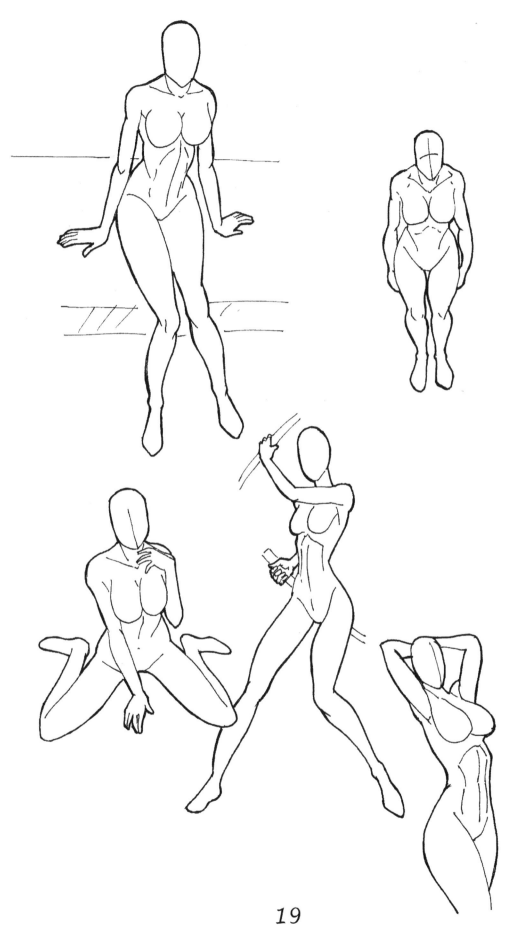

19

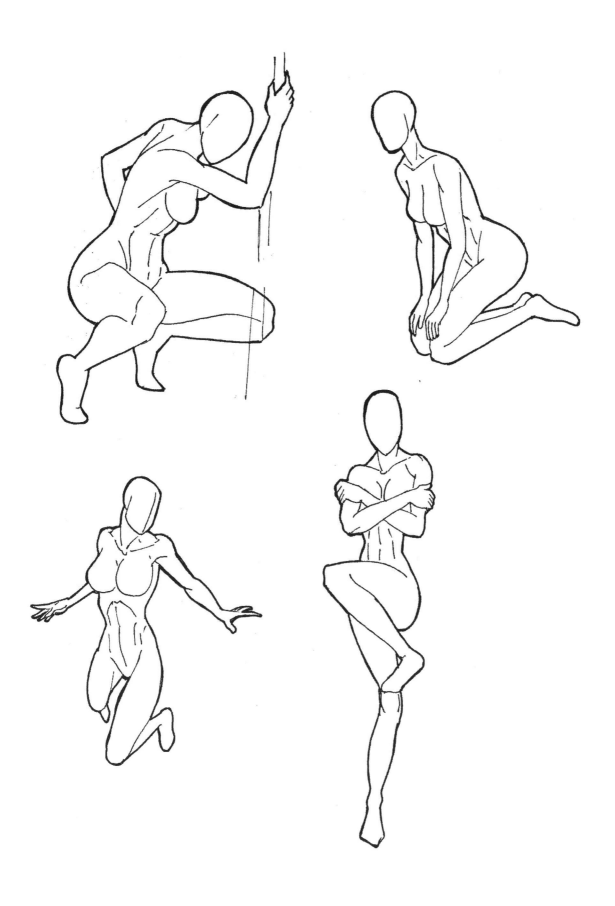

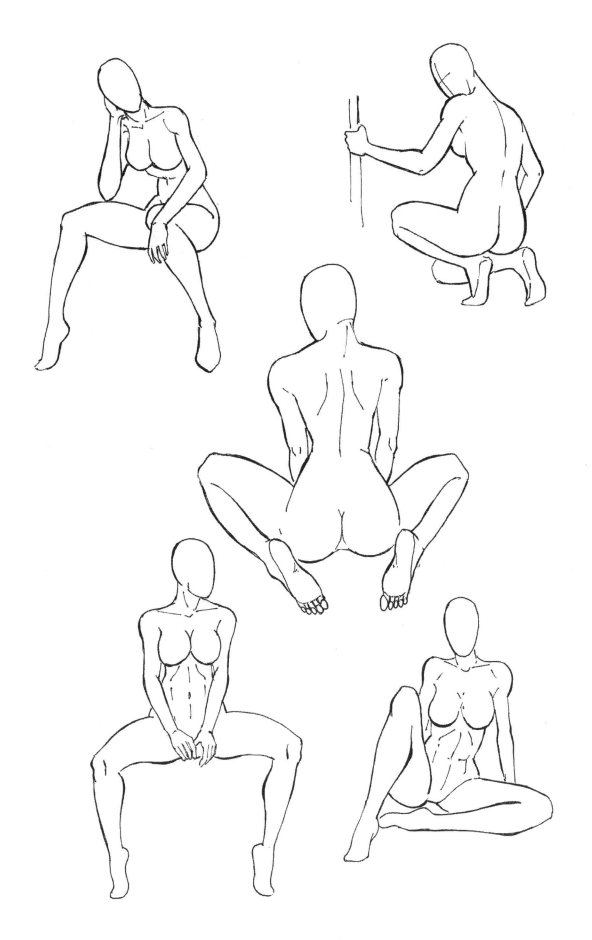

26

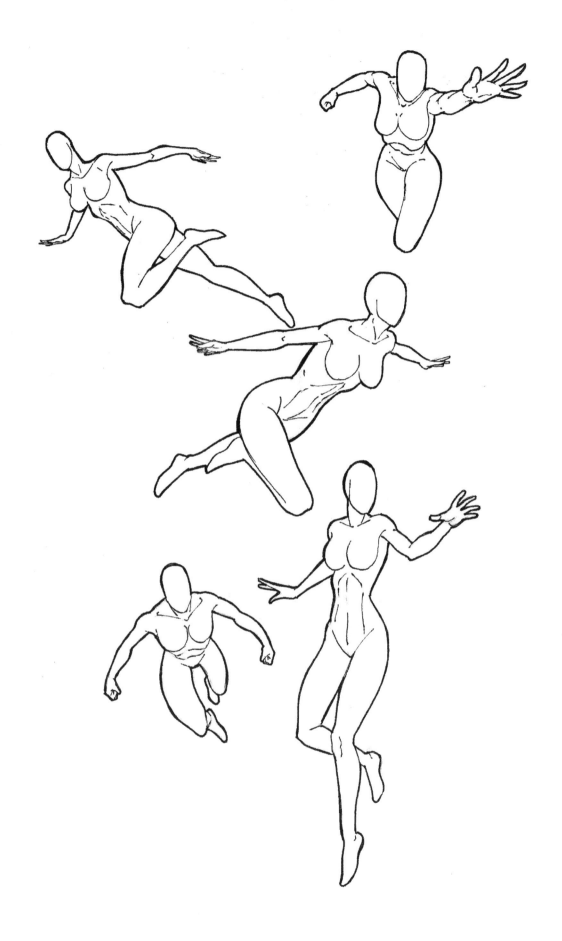

29

31

Made in the USA
Monee, IL
30 March 2023